Welcome to my first coloring book! I know you don't always feel like coloring the same thing all the time. So I drew a variety of pages with different patterns, shapes, and designs.

Simply color each page or make it completely unique. Try adding new combinations of colors or try adding different designs. You can even add words, names, quotes, or phrases. Don't worry about making a mistake. I added a place for you to try out all of your ideas before you add them to your favorite pages.

You can keep this as a coloring book, turn it into a journal, or even frame your favorite pages when you're done. Whatever you choose, make it your own because this book belongs to you!

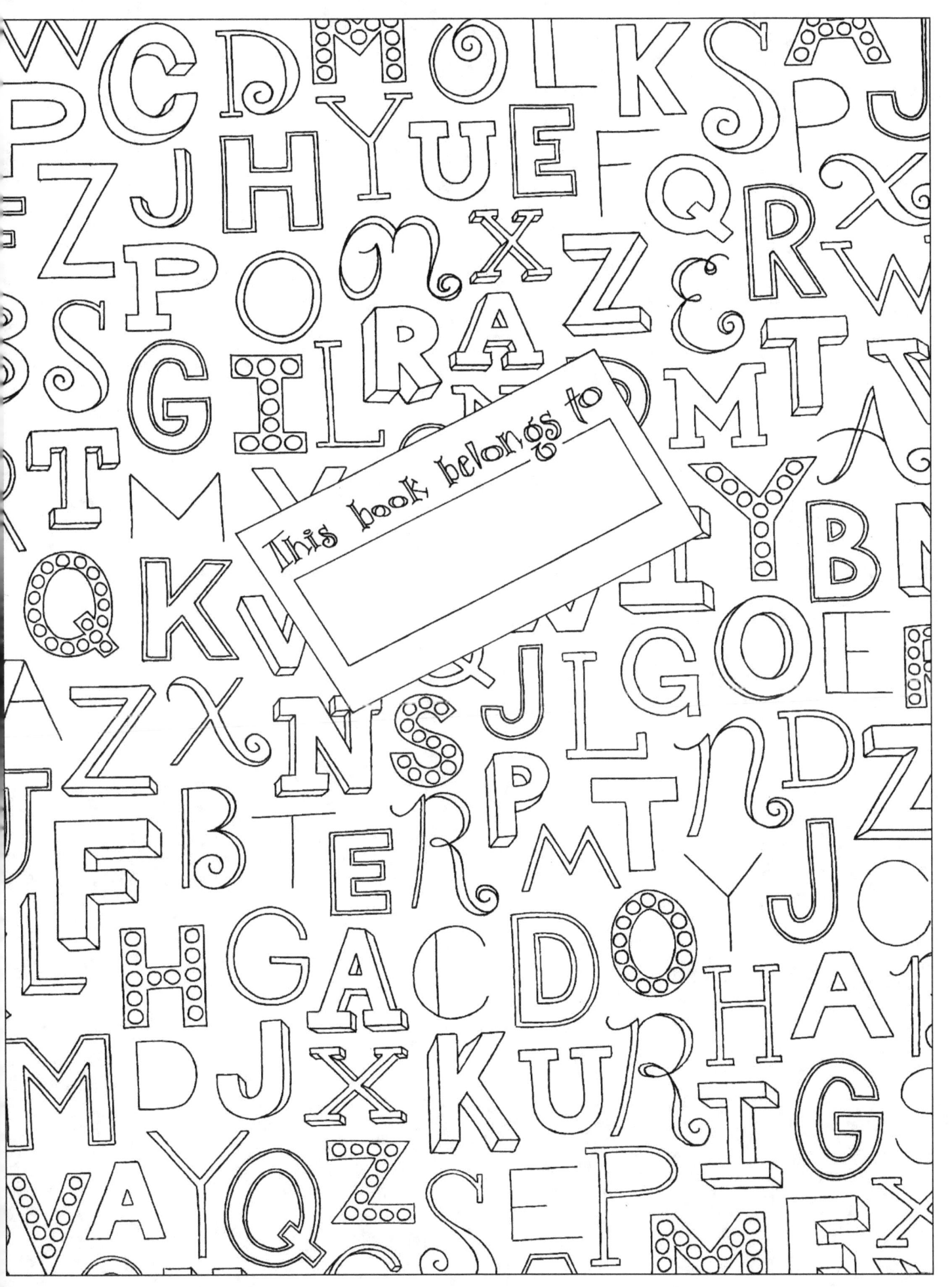

This book belongs to

Try Out Your Materials (color & test page)

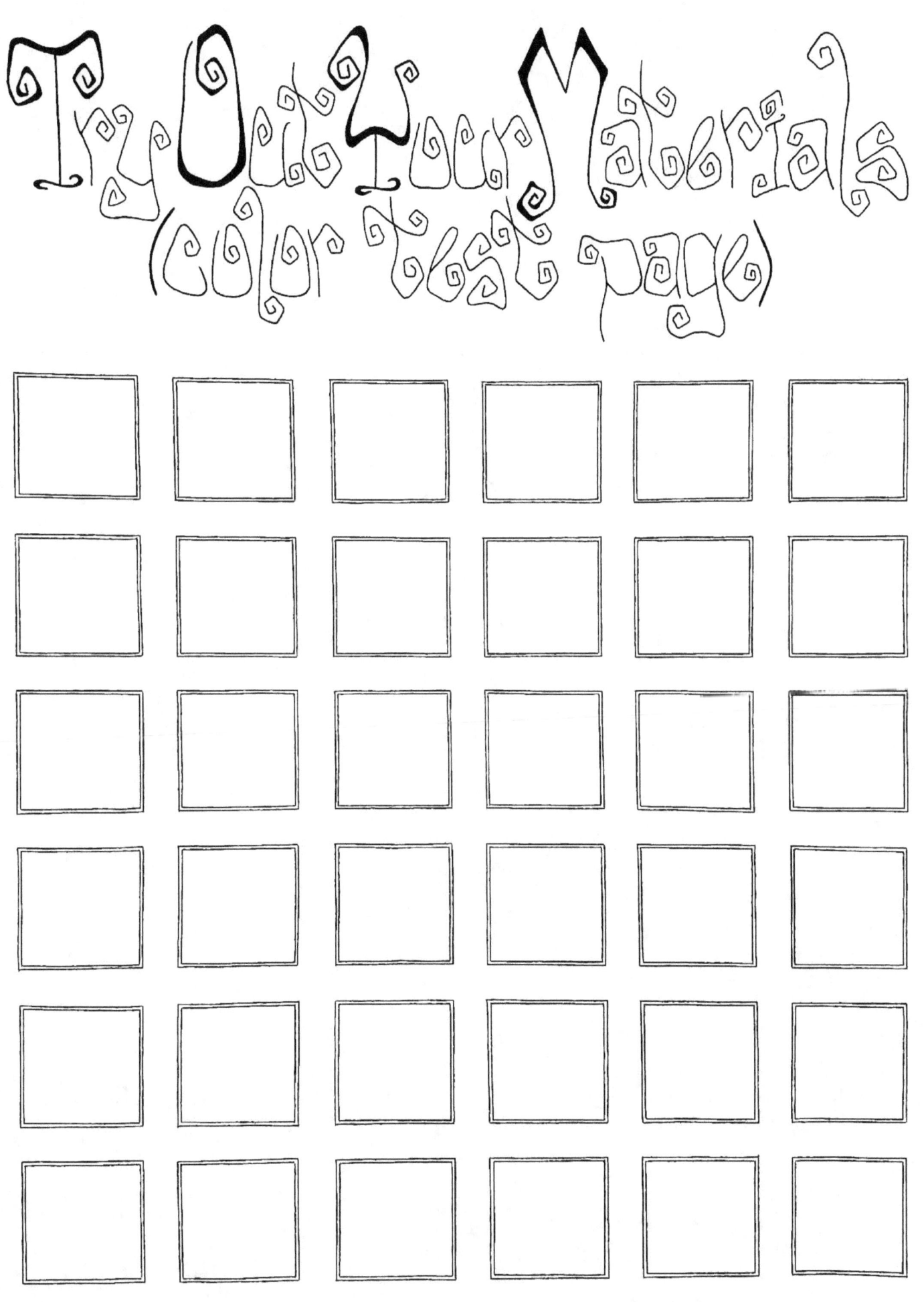

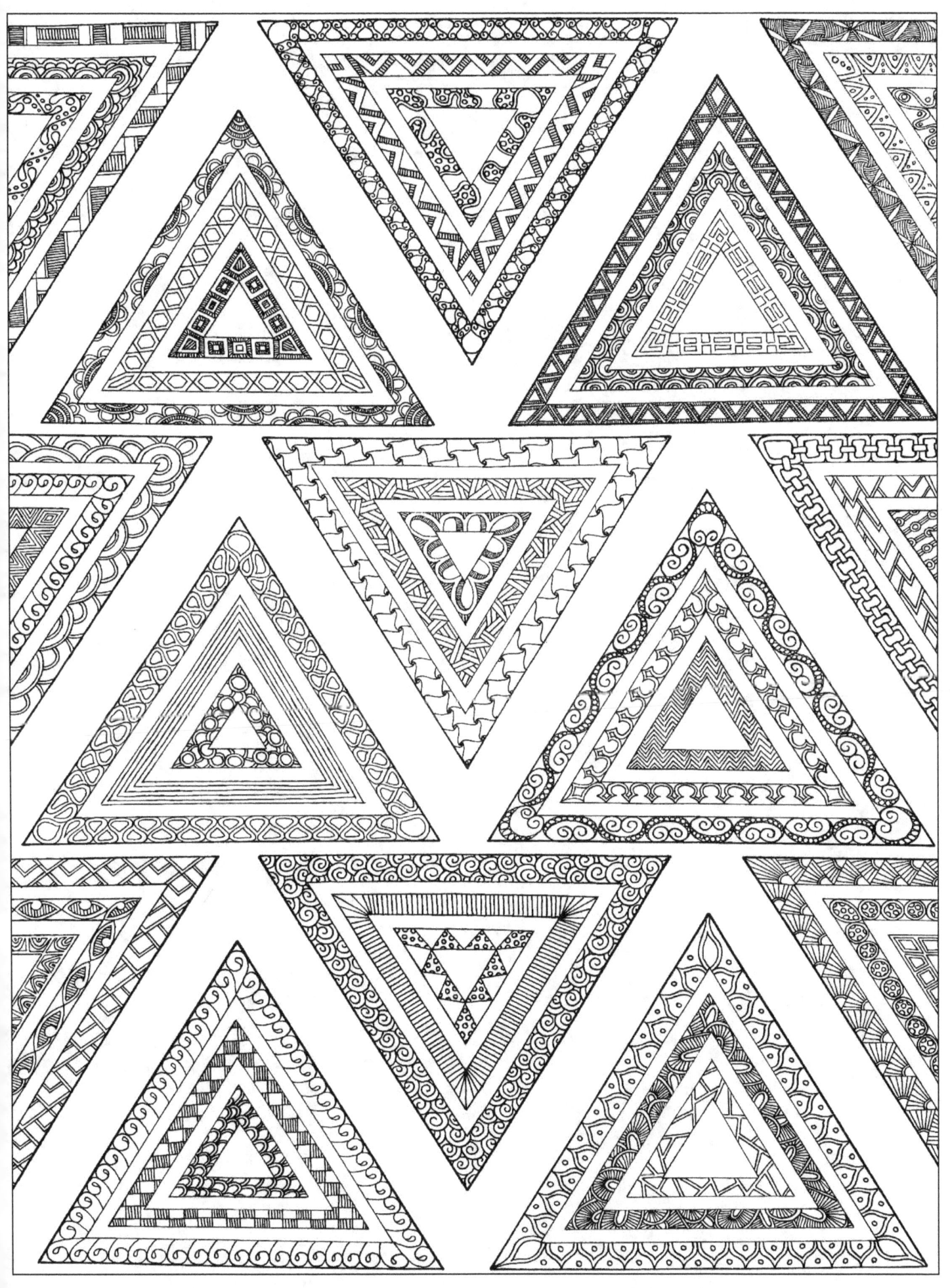

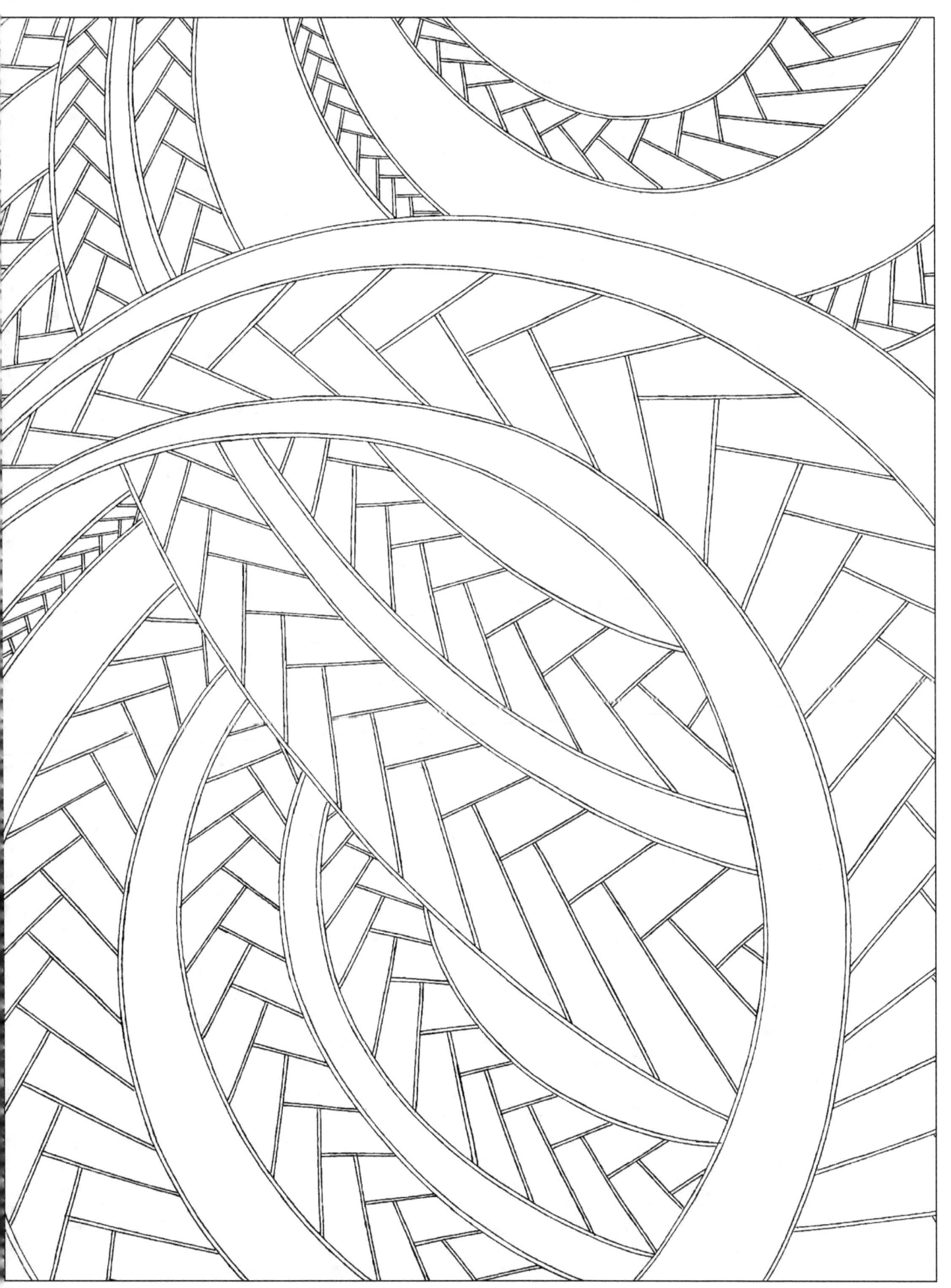

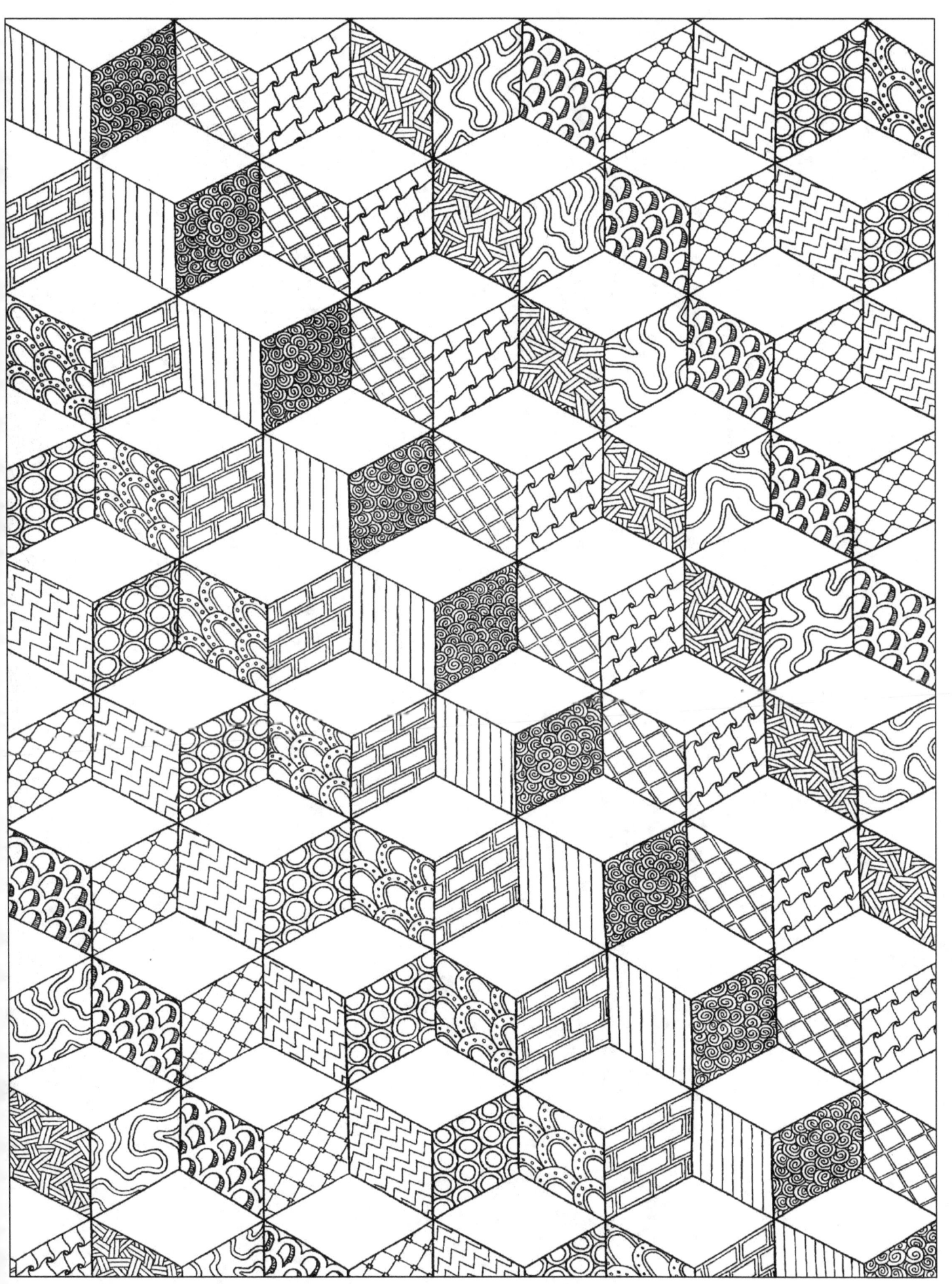

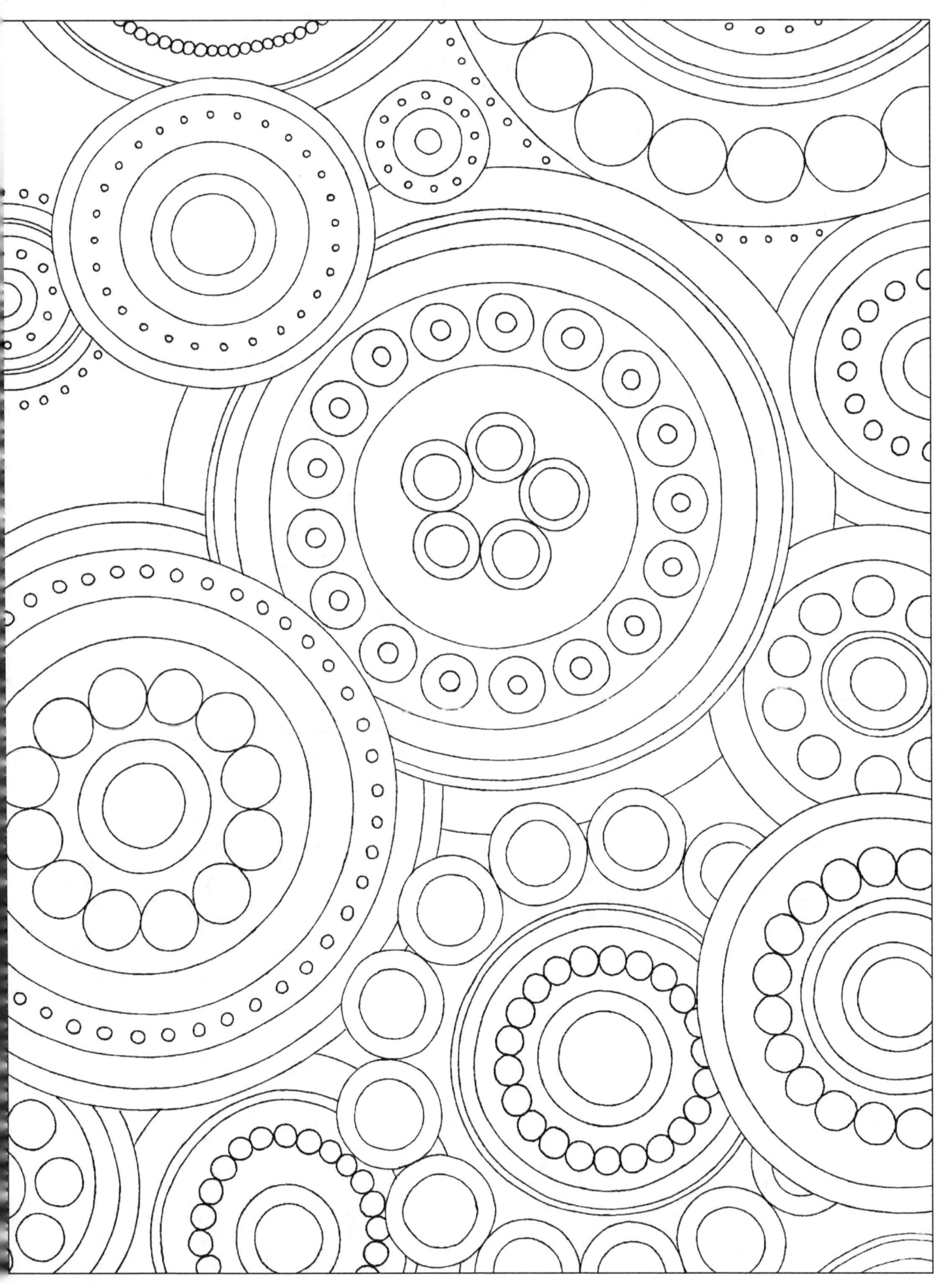

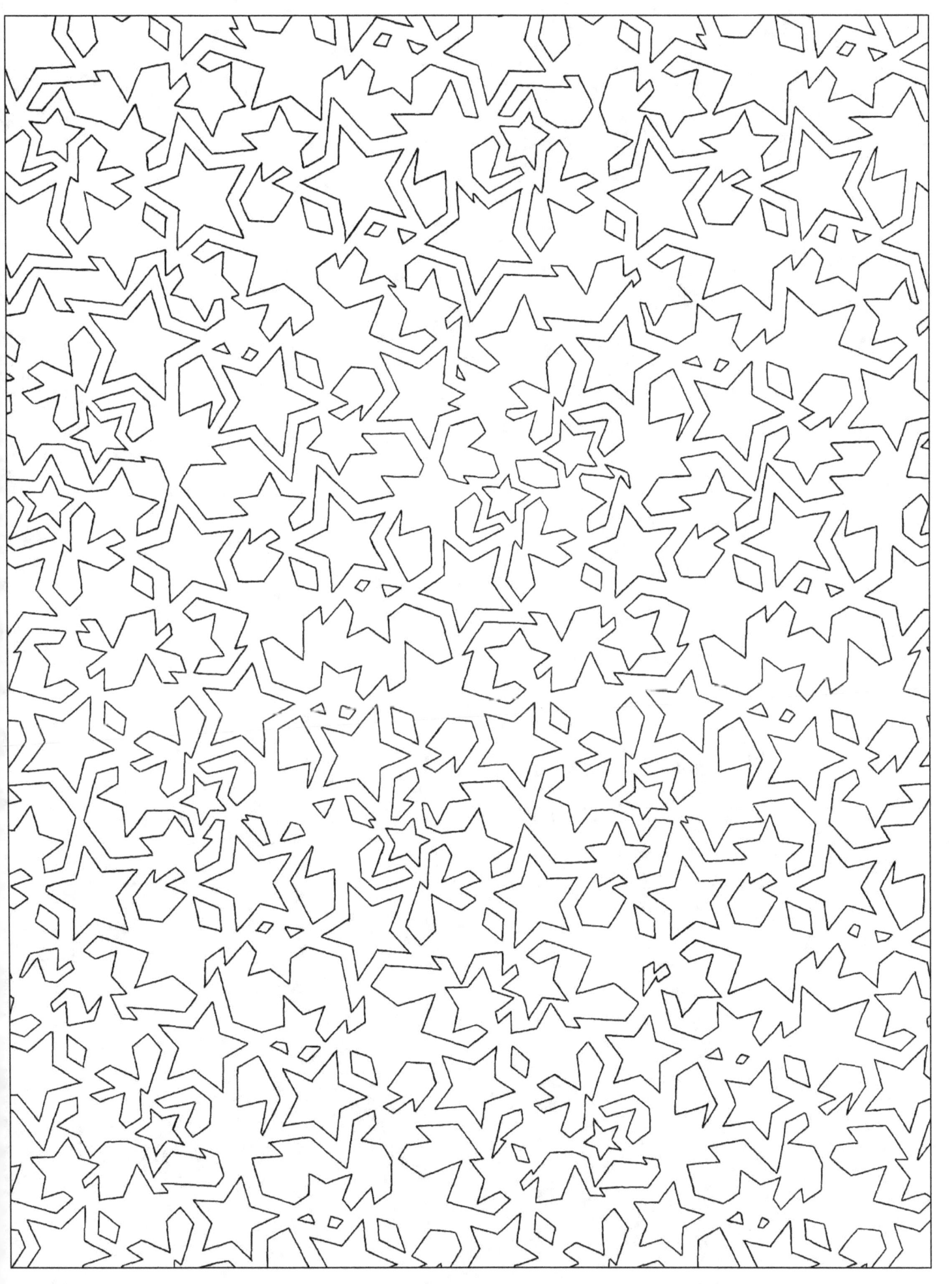

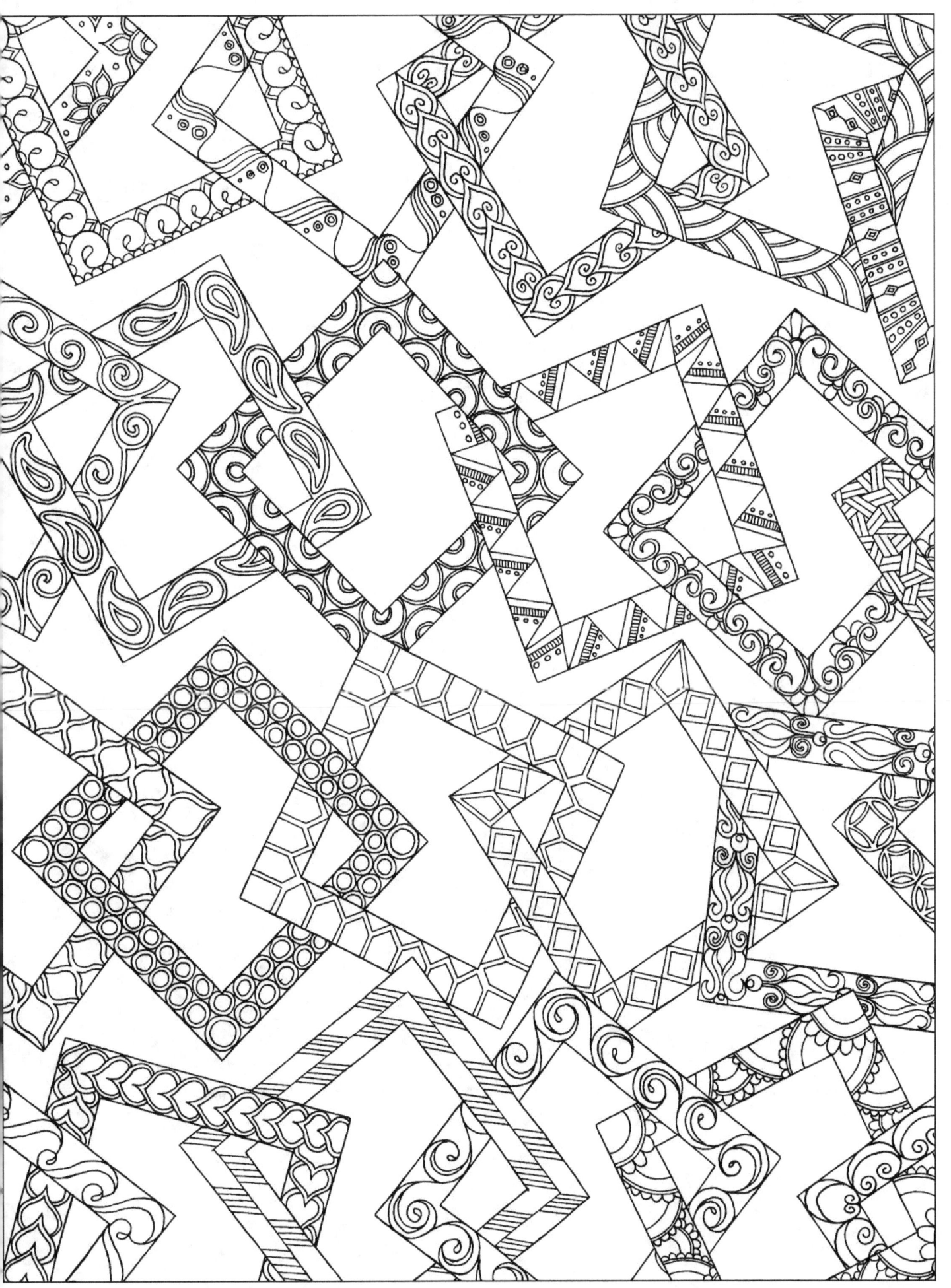

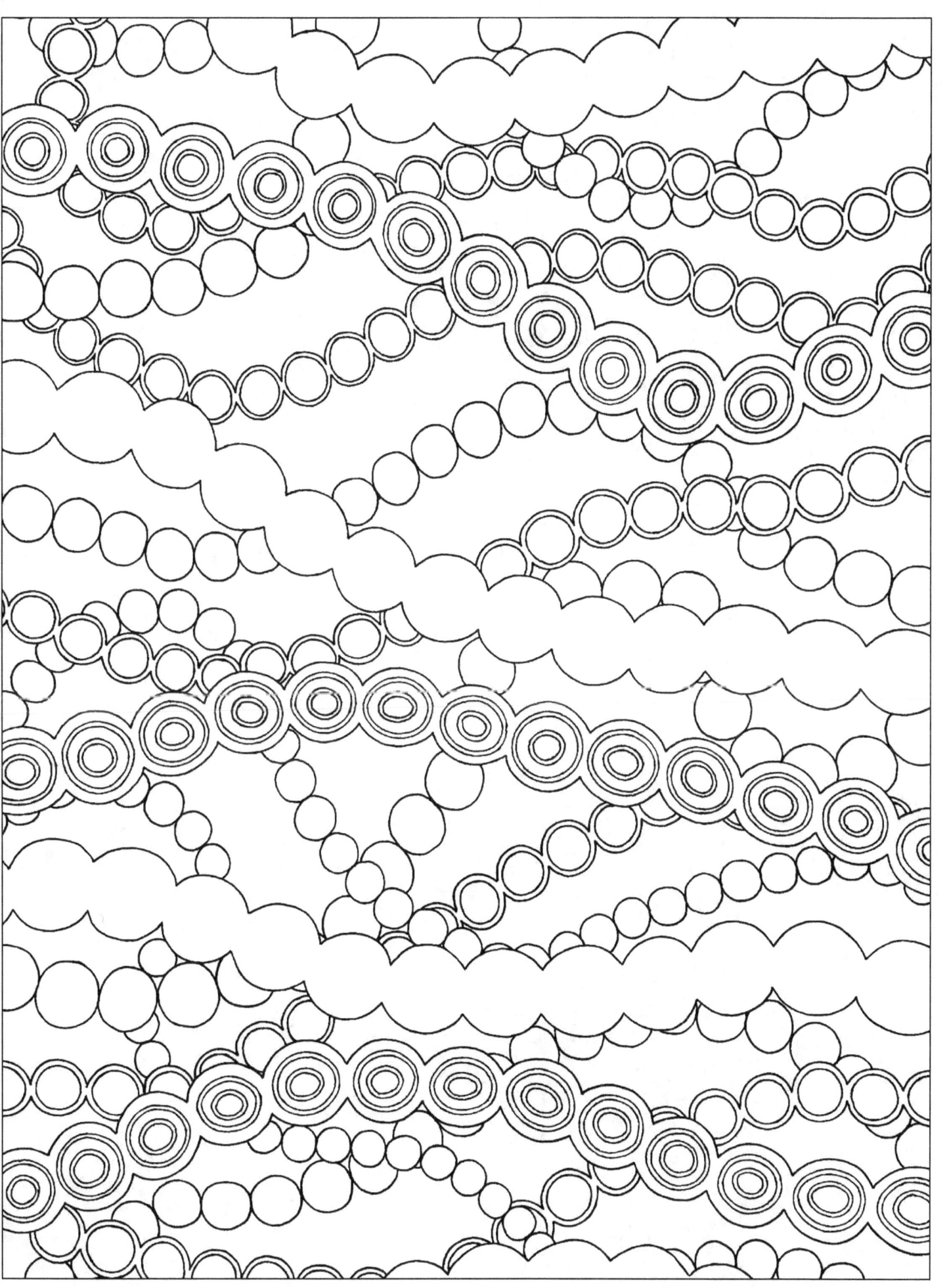

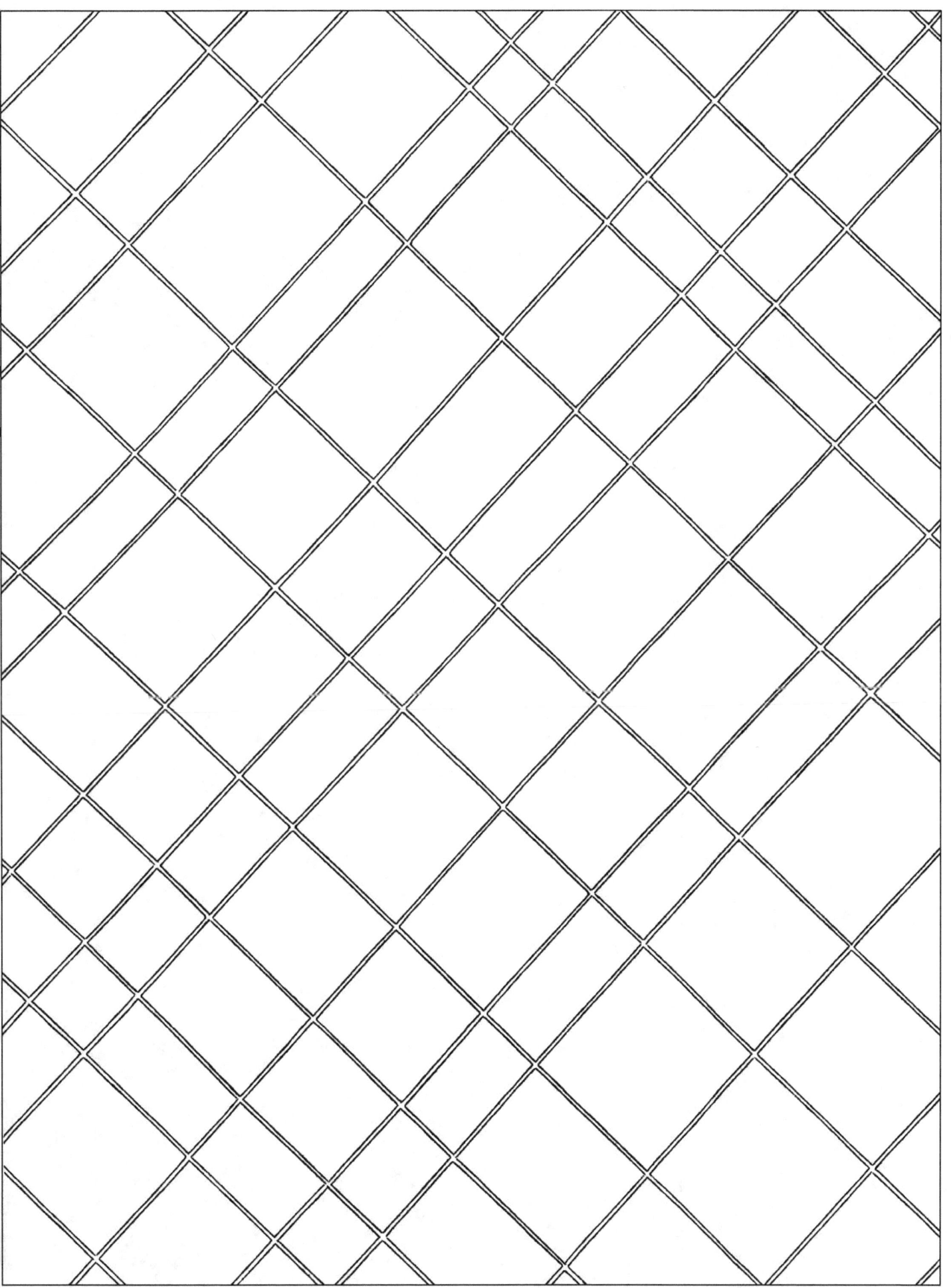

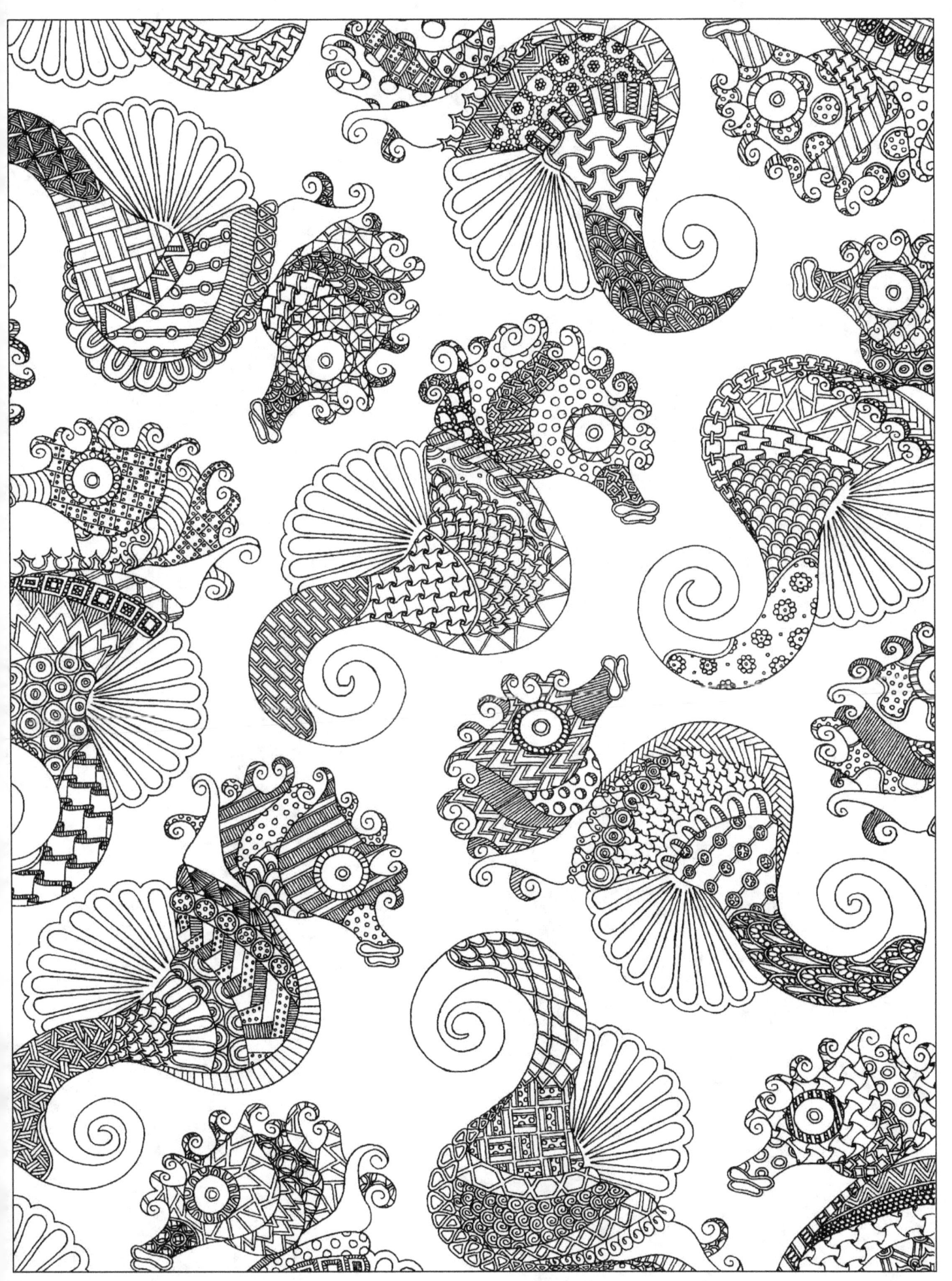

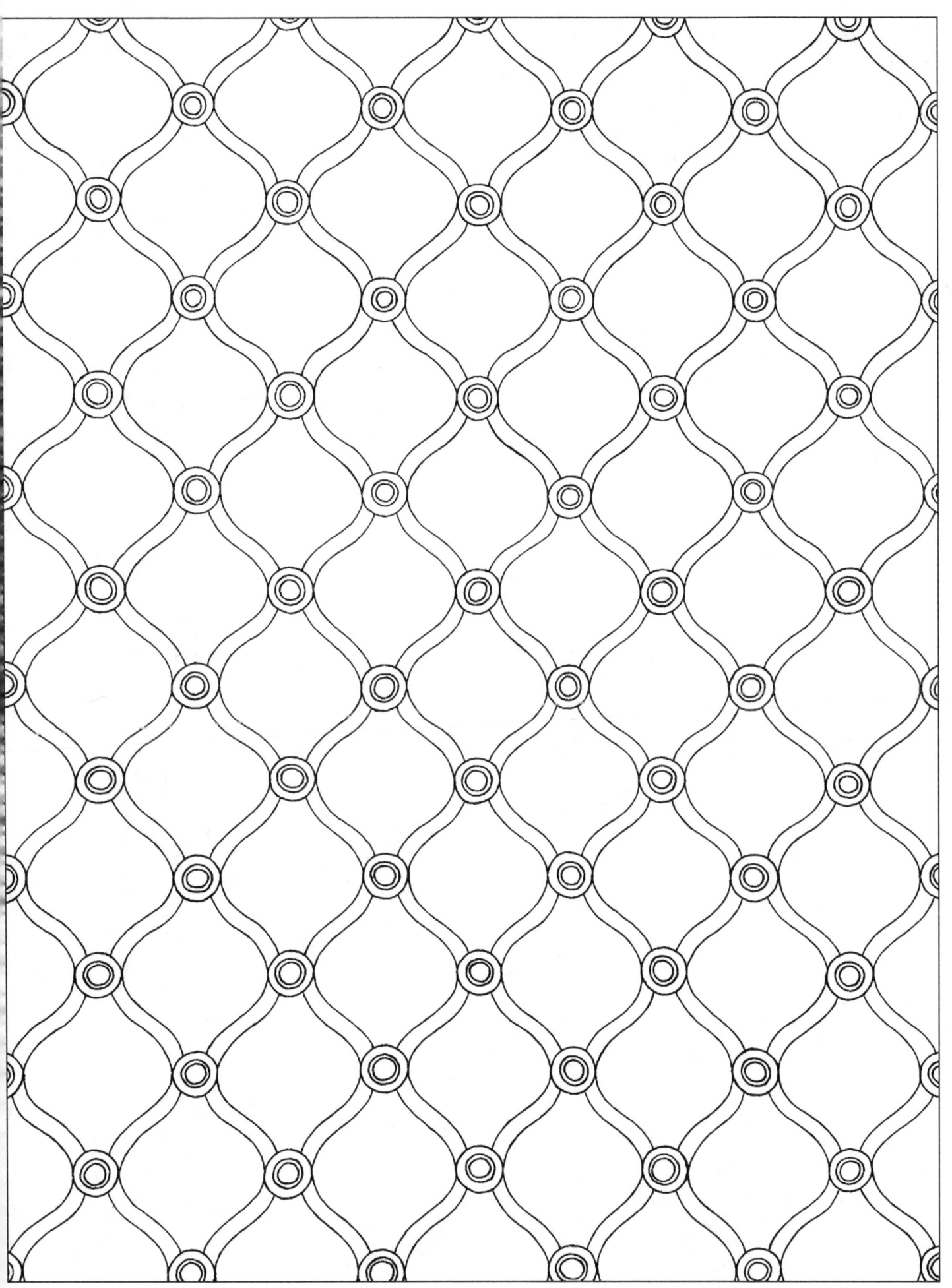

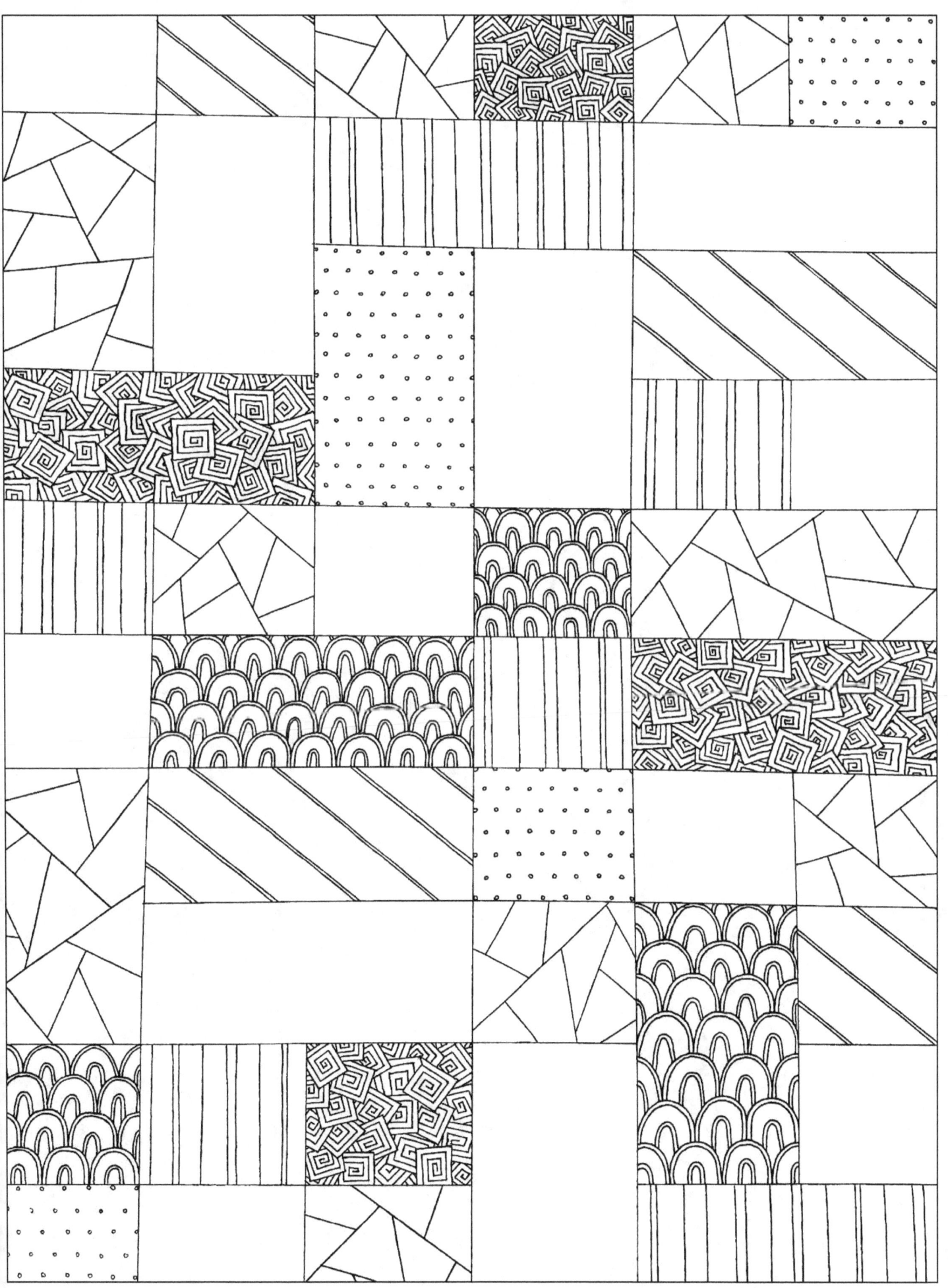

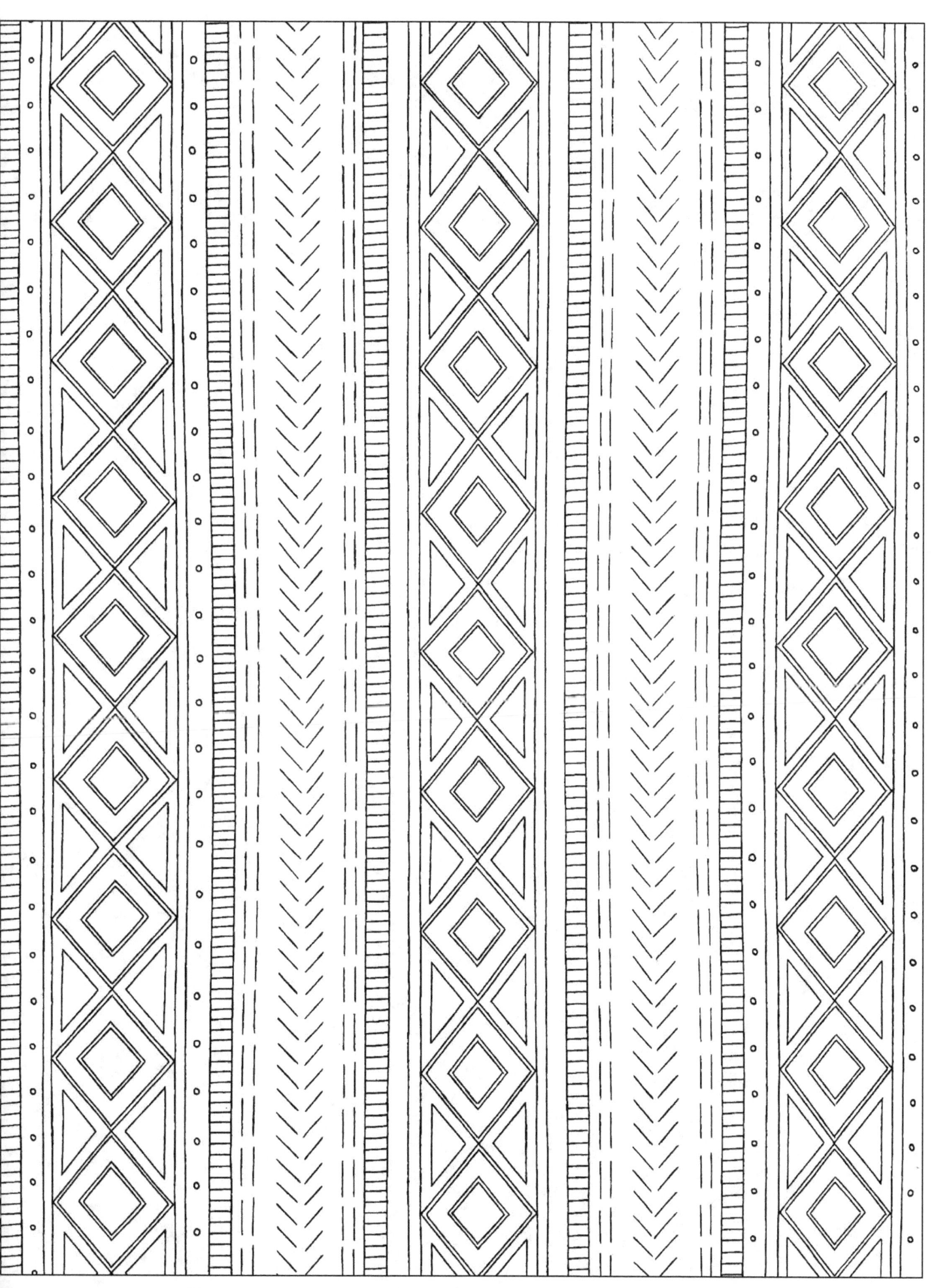

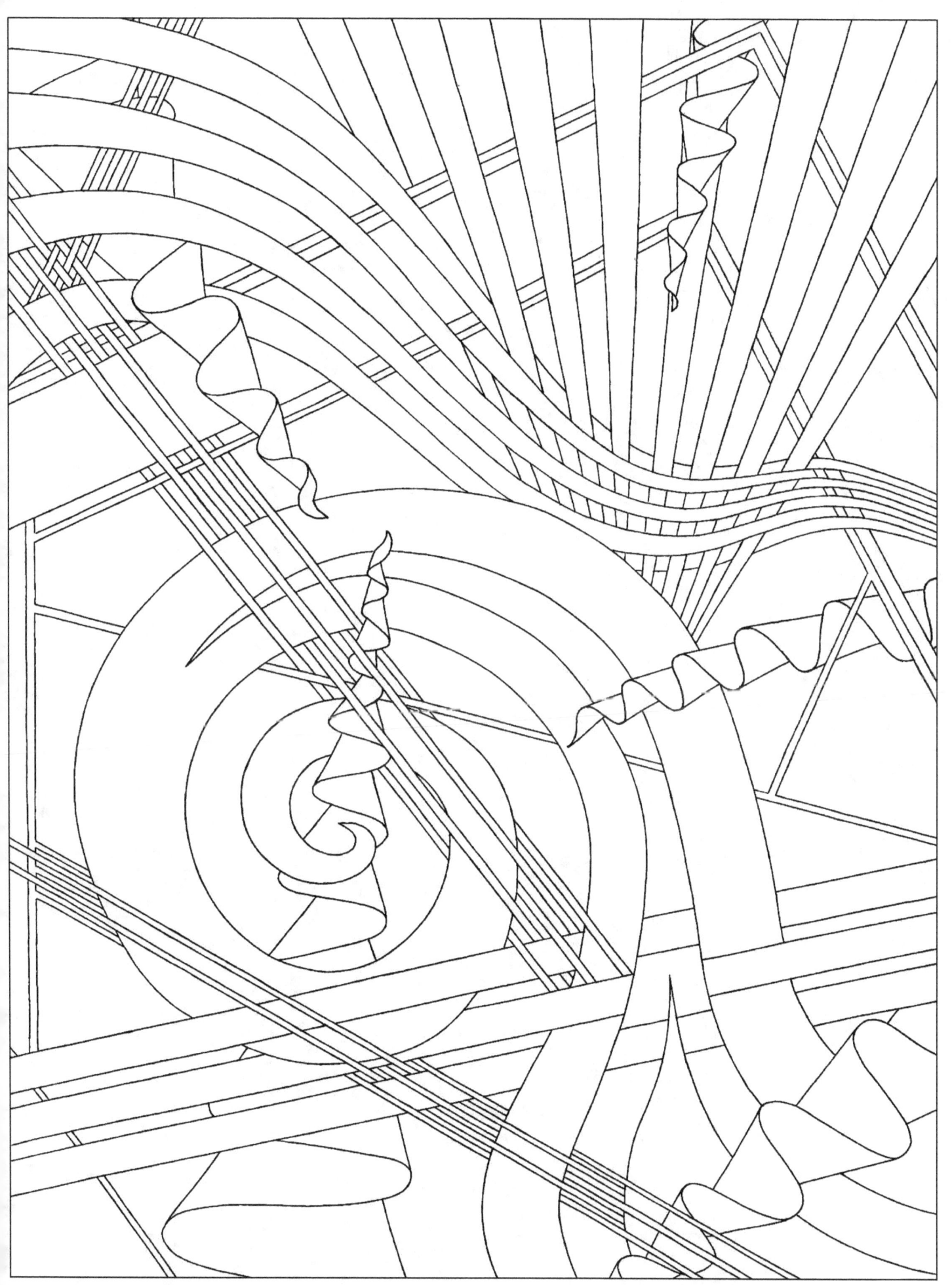

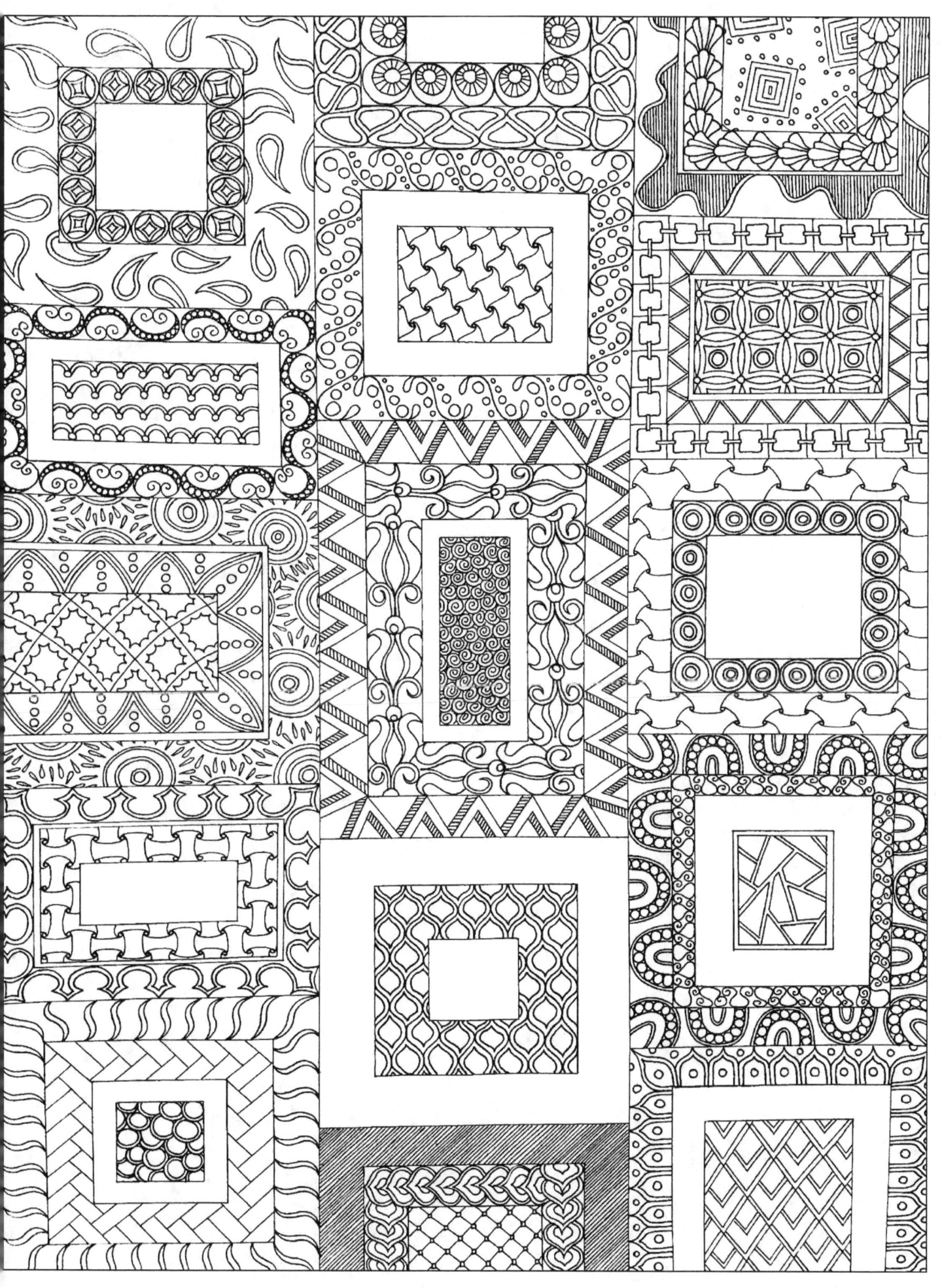

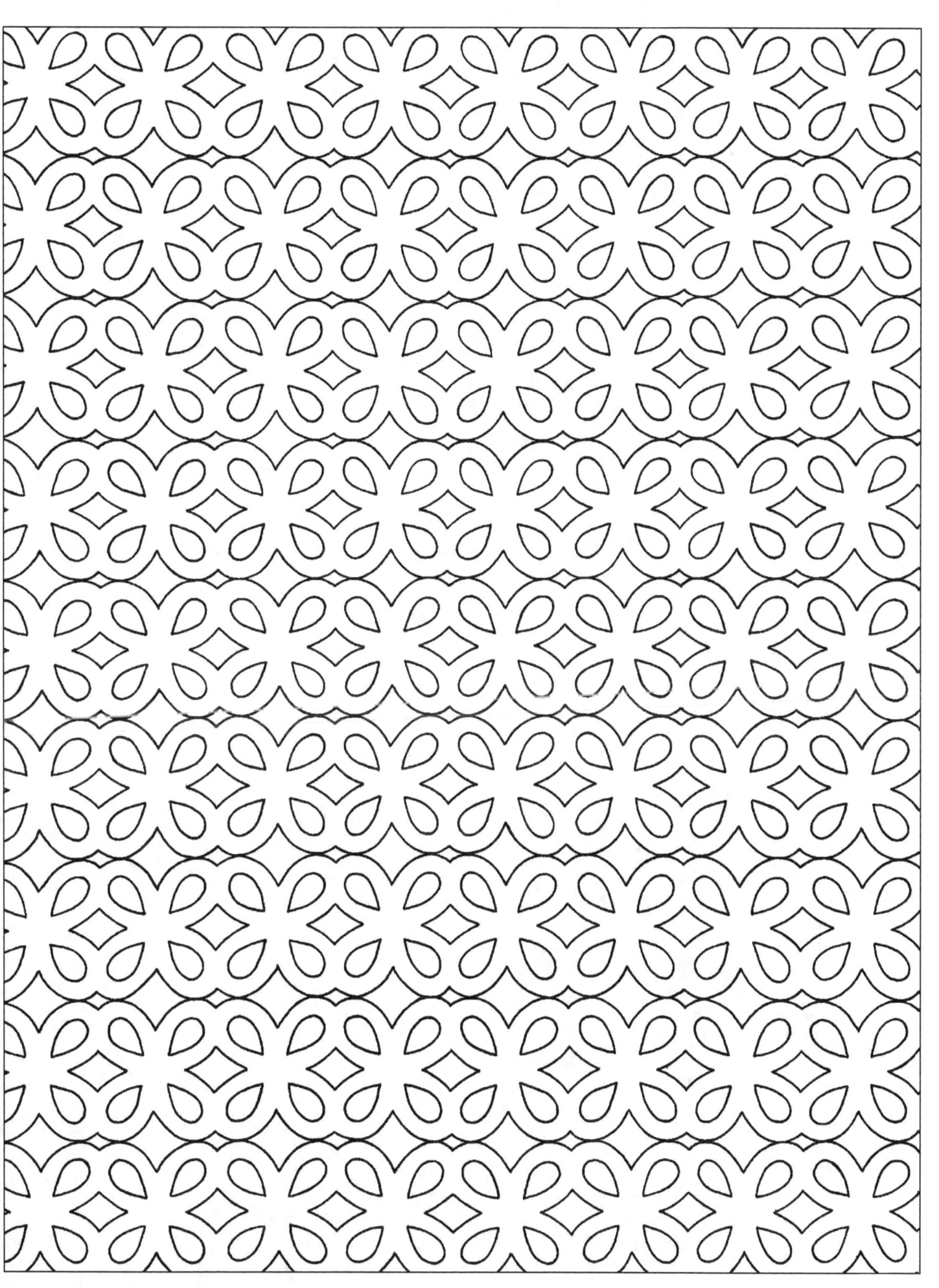

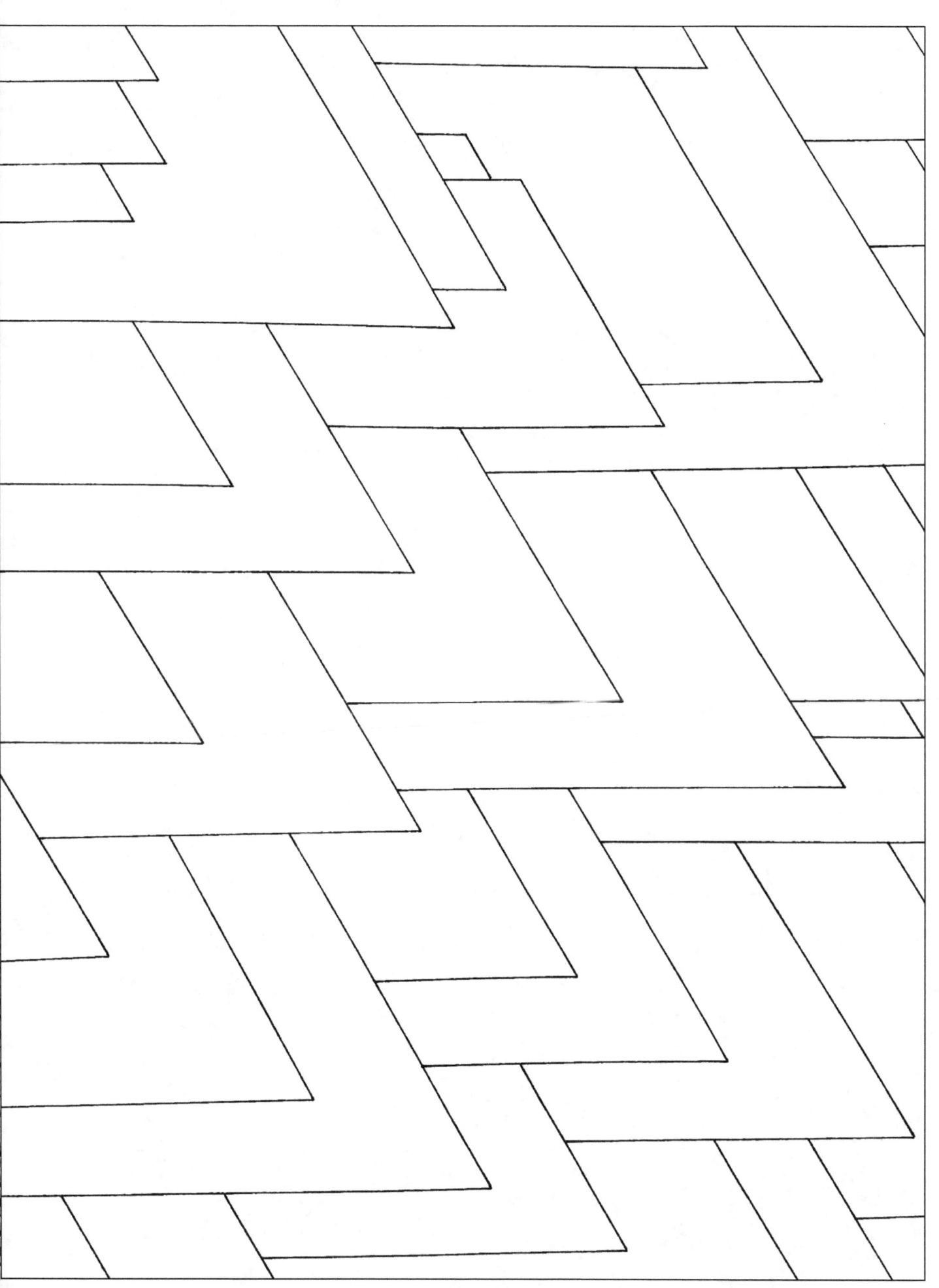

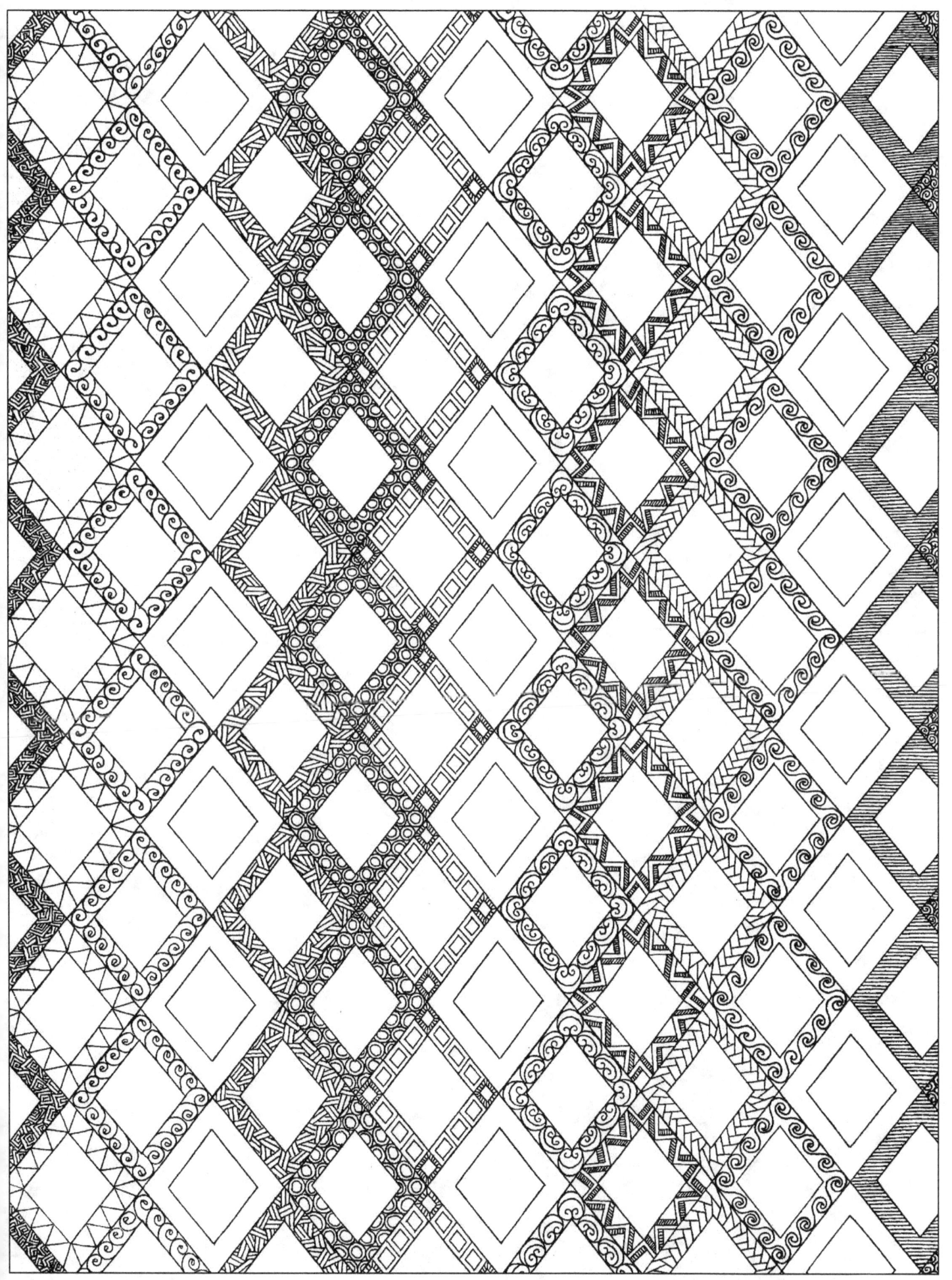

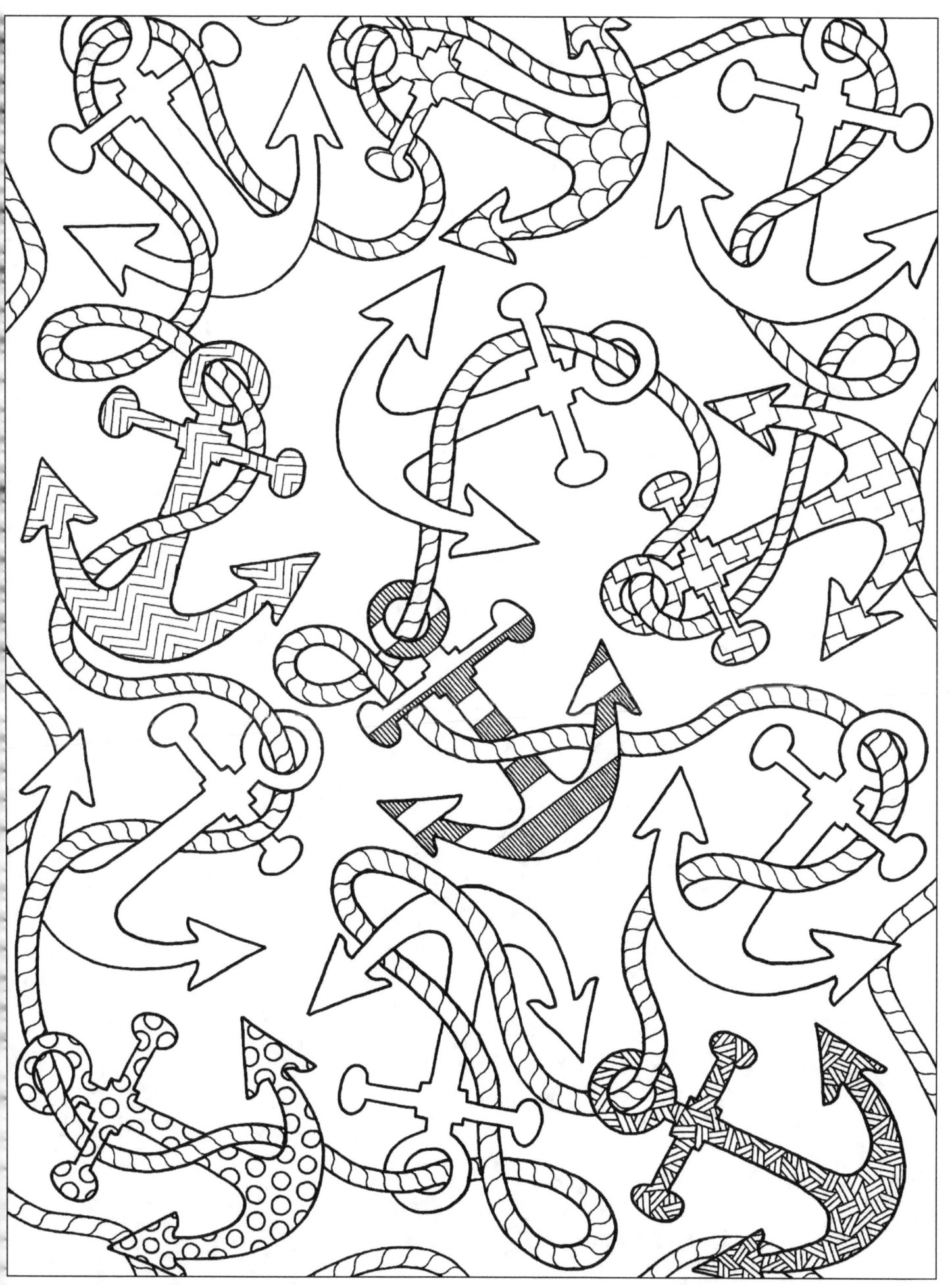

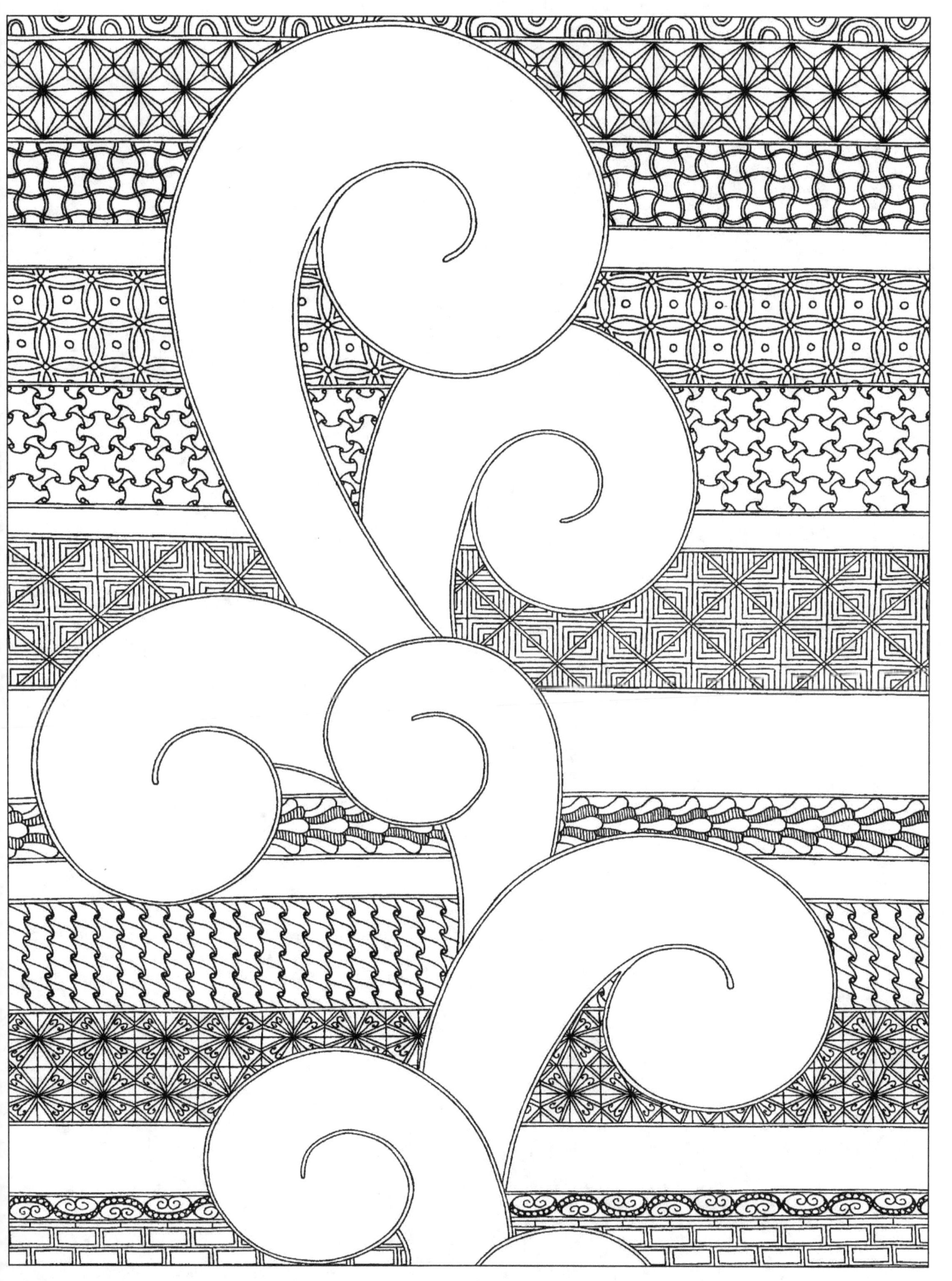

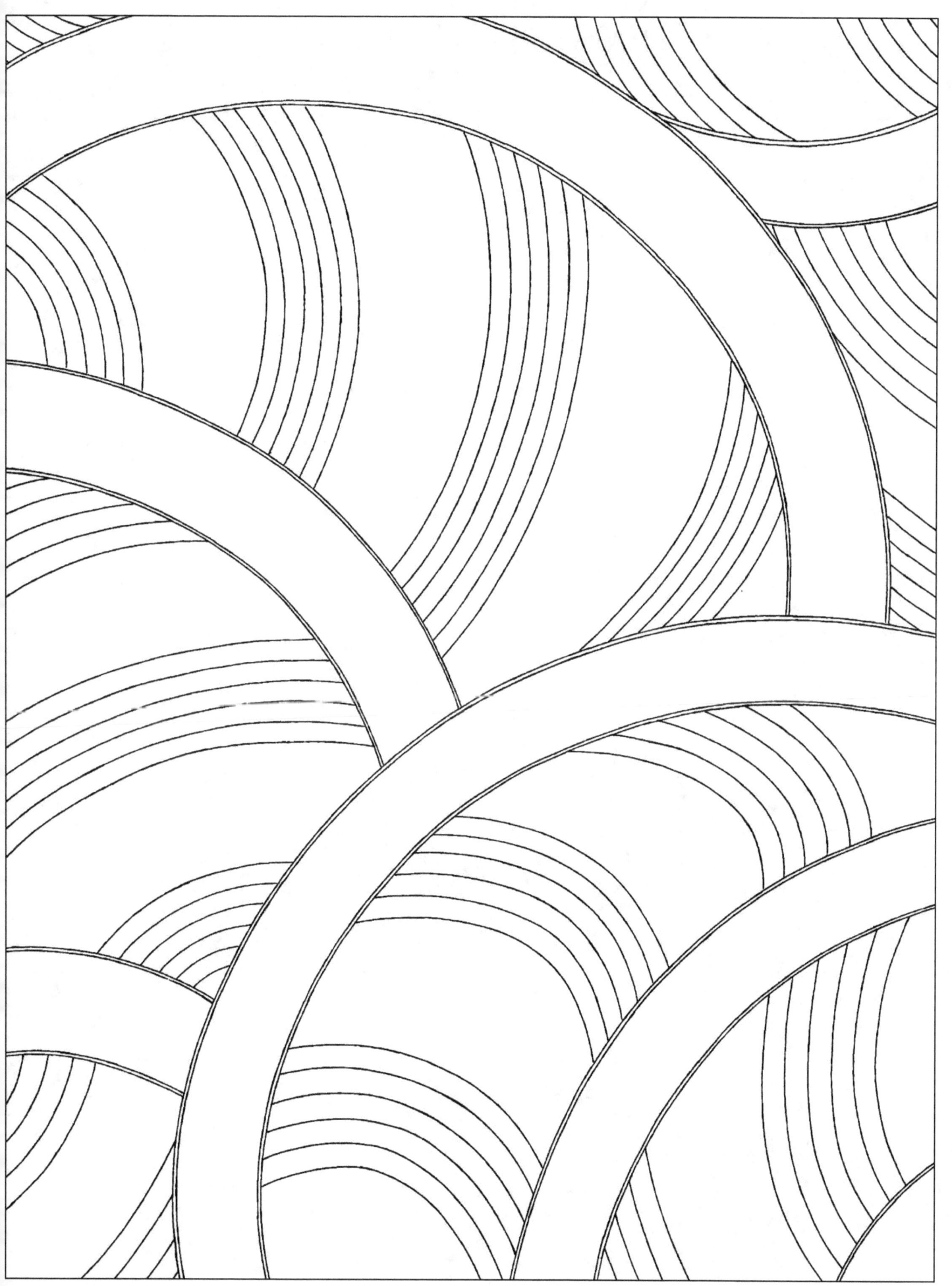

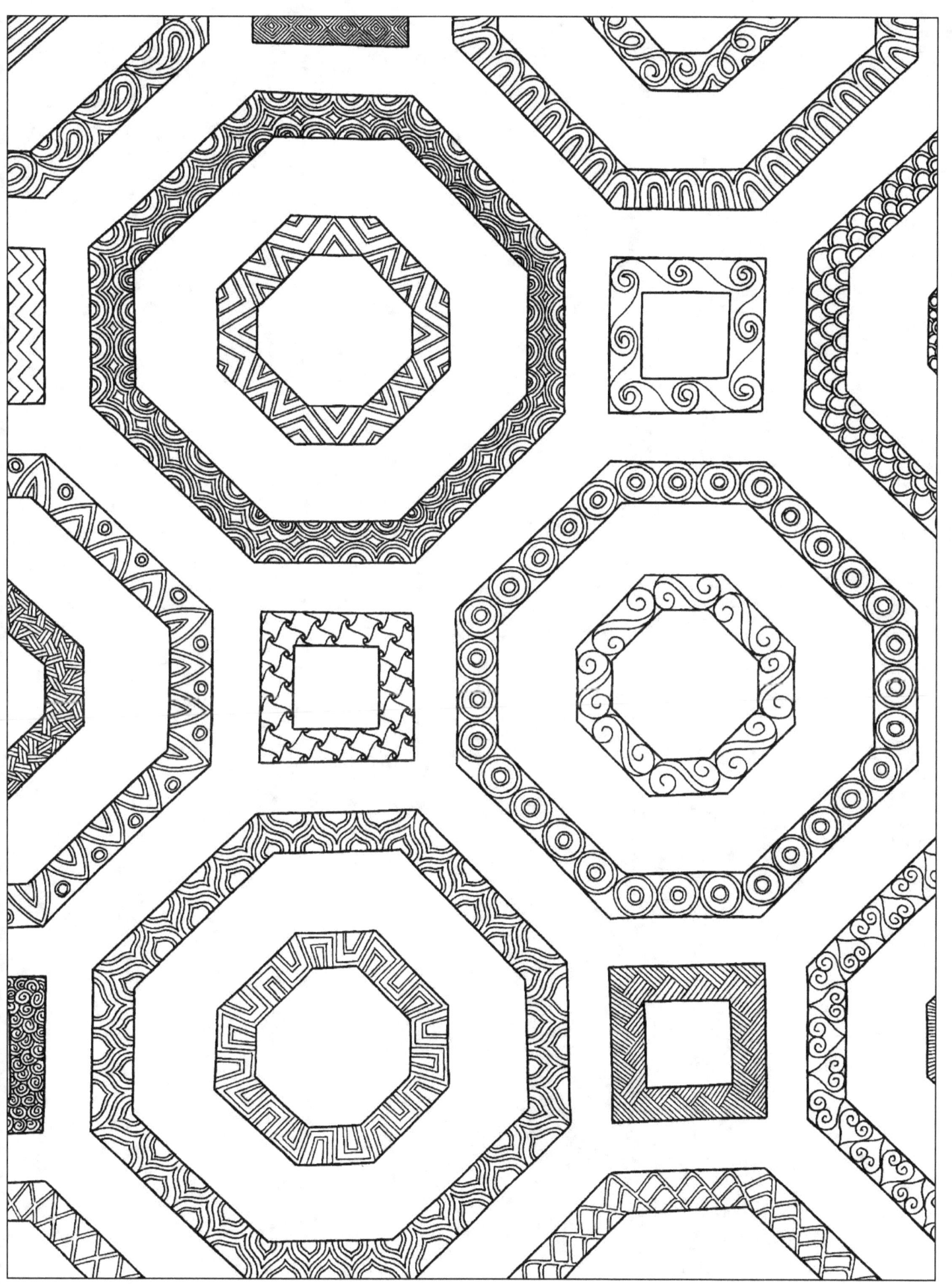

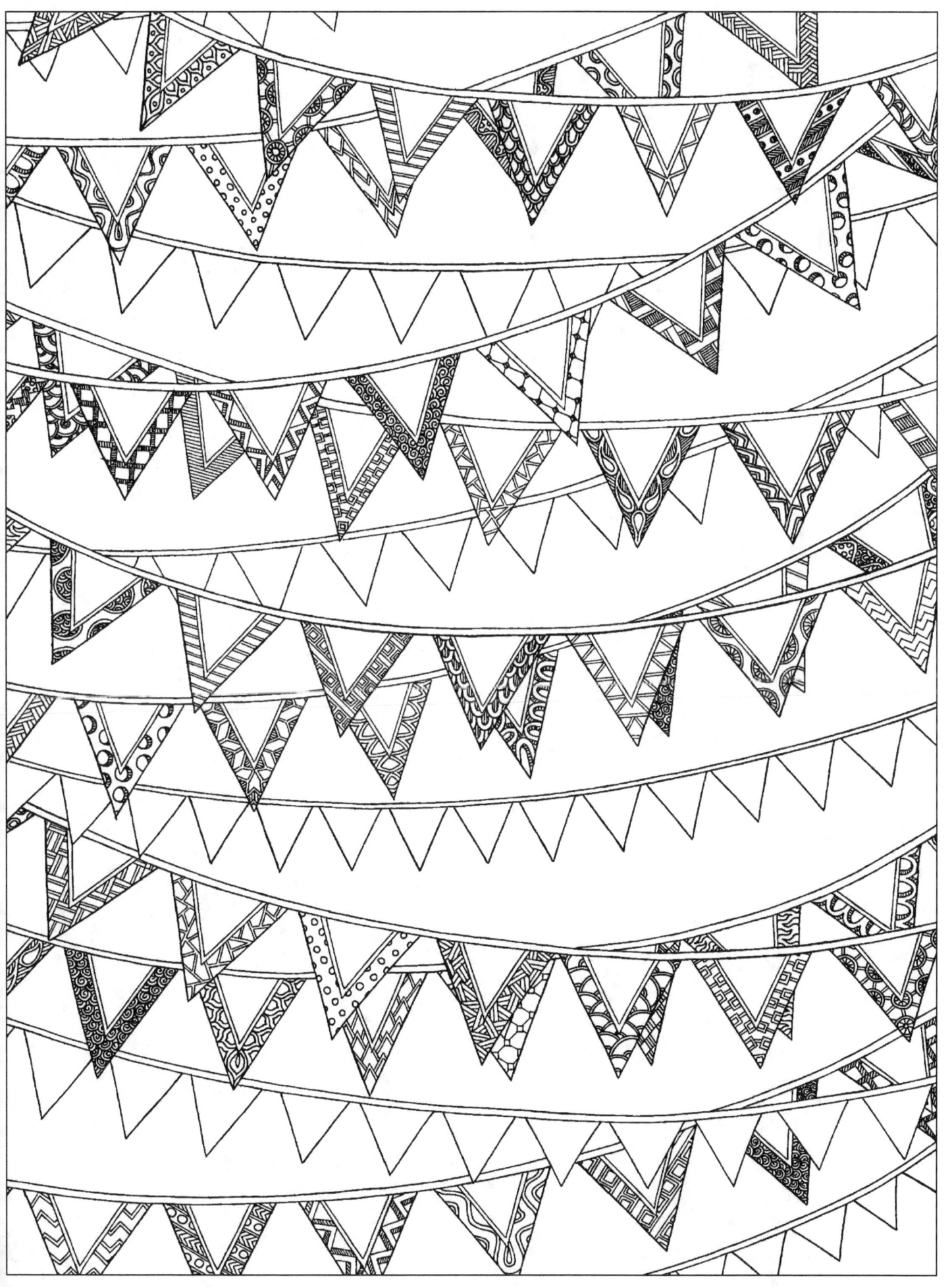

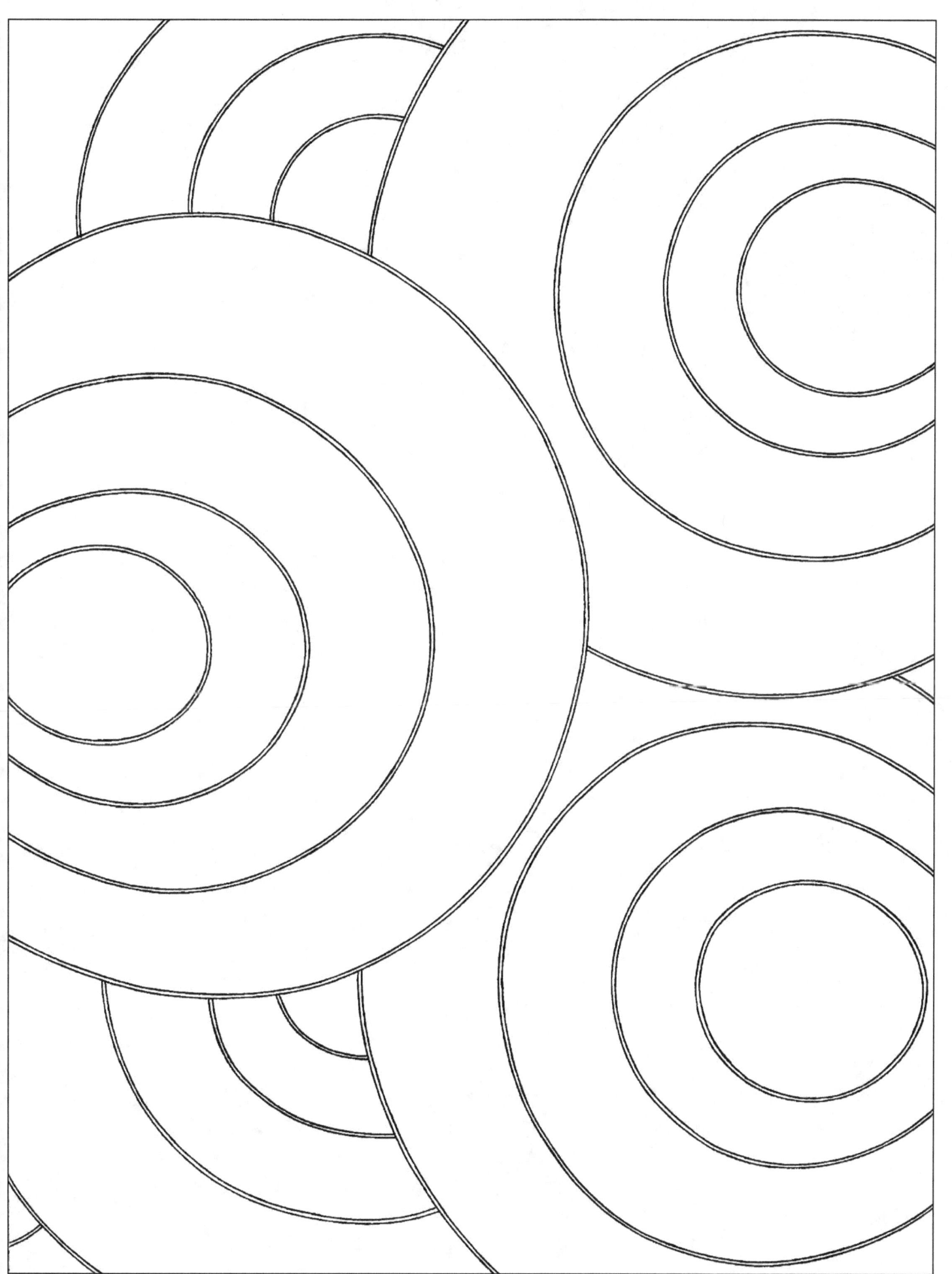

I want to say thank you to my amazing husband. I wouldn't have been able to do this without your patience, support, and encouragement.

I hope you have enjoyed making this book something that is uniquely yours!

Which pages were your favorite? What kind of things would you like to see in my next coloring book? Send an email to ThisColoringBookBelongsToYou@gmail.com and don't forget to leave a review on Amazon!

Lindsey

www.ingramcontent.com/pod-product-compliance
Lightning Source LLC
Chambersburg PA
CBHW081639220526

45468CB00009B/2500